D1648469

Stop
Depriving
the
World
of You

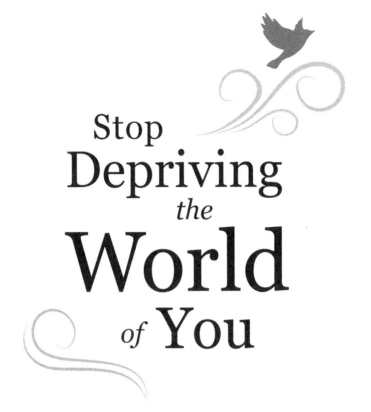

Stop Depriving the World of You

A Guide for Getting Unstuck

DARLENE M. CORBETT

© Copyright 2018–Darlene Corbett.

All rights reserved. This book is protected by the copyright laws of the United States of America. This book may not be copied or reprinted for commercial gain or profit. The use of short quotations or occasional page copying for personal or group study is permitted and encouraged. Permission will be granted upon request. For permissions requests, write to the publisher, addressed "Attention: Permissions Coordinator," at the address below.

SOUND WISDOM
P.O. Box 310
Shippensburg, PA 17257-0310

For more information on publishing and distribution rights, call 717-530-2122 or info@soundwisdom.com.

Quantity Sales. Special discounts are available on quantity purchases by corporations, associations, and others. For details, contact the Sales Department at Sound Wisdom.

While efforts have been made to verify information contained in this publication, neither the author nor the publisher assumes any responsibility for errors, inaccuracies, or omissions.

While this publication is chock-full of useful, practical information, it is not intended to be legal or accounting advice. All readers are advised to seek competent lawyers and accountants to follow laws and regulations that may apply to specific situations.

The reader of this publication assumes responsibility for the use of the information. The author and publisher assume no responsibility or liability whatsoever on the behalf of the reader of this publication.

ISBN 13 TP: 978-1-64095-028-3
ISBN 13 Ebook: 978-1-64095-029-0

For Worldwide Distribution, Printed in the U.S.A.
1 2 3 4 5 6 7 8 / 21 20 19 18

Cover/Jacket designer Eileen Rockwell
Interior design by Susan Ramundo

I dedicate this book to my husband, Steven Hyjek;
my longtime friend and consultant,
Sandra Talanian; and in memory of my spirited
mother, Dolores, and sweet father, Michael,
who I firmly believe are smiling from afar.

"Whatever the mind can conceive and believe, it can achieve."—Napoleon Hill

Contents

CHAPTER 1

Get Unstuck: All Living Specimens Are in Movement

Have you ever really thought about the fact that the universe is constantly in flux? That's right! Nothing truly stays the same. If you have never given this much reflection, take a few moments to focus on this idea. Although such shifting is not always visible to the human eye, there is movement all around us. Often, we take it for granted. The earth rotates around the sun, but we do not feel it. The seasons change, and we see it as part of life, except for those of us in the northeast who grumble about humid summers and freezing winters.

Without thinking about movement, we come to appreciate the gifts we receive from such activity.

Beautiful perennials begin their arrival at spring's doorstep, reminding us that the dry heat of summer is right around the corner. Glorious autumn ushers in a unique display of colors, and although many of us eventually tire of the cold and snow, some people, especially skiers, enjoy winter wonderland.

What about the animals? They instinctively recognize the times of the year to accelerate their movement. Robins head south for the winter along with other species including many human snowbirds. The Monarch butterfly is an example of movement and change at its most spectacular. They leave their caterpillar body through metamorphosis and become the most majestic of winged insects before moving to warmer climates.

All four classical elements exhibit movement. The earth is constantly shifting, but so subtly as not to upset nature, except on rare occasions when we experience deadly earthquakes. The air is moving, as creatures of the earth breathe in oxygen and expel carbon dioxide. For those who study the sun, movement happens along its surface. Finally, water, magnificent H_2O in its fluid state, abounds with motion. Even when frozen, under the right conditions, movement prevails.

Now you might wonder, why I am discussing such an esoteric issue? Should this not be left to philosophers, climatologists or perhaps biologists or other scientists who are interested in the impact of movement on us? For the average Joe or Josephine, does it really matter? People are so busy with their own lives they might simply say, "Who cares! What does this have to do with me?" I would look at them and say, "Everything and anything related to you and your world." They might look at me with a perplexed expression, but not desire to continue the dialogue. Others might yawn, look bored and change the subject or even walk away, but what about those who don't? They begin to ponder this idea as something worth exploring. If you fall in that last category, I am talking about you. Yes, right again, you, the one who is open to possibilities and willing to explore the idea of movement and its influence on your life journey. My desire to write this book is for you! I want to share with you my belief in your ability to get unstuck and move beyond your current circumstances.

It is my ultimate belief that the ingenious author, George Eliot, was correct. "You are never too old to be what you might have been." I invite you to consider her words of wisdom. I also suggest you give my words pause: "The bad news is that nothing stays the same, but the better news is nothing stays the same." The impermanence of each moment gives us opportunity for growth and transformation. With each slight shift, change can occur, and that, my friend, is a wonderful thing! Each of us should keep this in mind all the days of our lives.

I hope you are ready to awaken the gifts, talents, and strengths that are lying dormant in you. Maybe you have started this process but lost momentum. Either way, you have already begun the exercise of getting unstuck and back on the right path. Let's get going! Be prepared for a fun and exciting adventure. Let me help you stop depriving the world of you, and watch what happens as you begin to sparkle and shine, from the inside out.

CHAPTER 2

Get Unstuck: You Are in Movement

Sometimes it feels as if you are in a rut and will never get out, so why bother trying? You believe that your efforts to do something different have gone by the wayside. Certain people seem to have it easier and just glide through life unencumbered. Sound familiar? Most people have these feelings at some time in their lives. There are even some people who believe certain situations remain permanent. One could make the argument for such a case, but what they forget is that what seems to be a permanent situation may have been a result of some change which continues to reverberate in one's life. Let me give you an example:

A few months ago, while in a nail salon of all places, I was discussing this very issue with a group of women.

Most agreed with me or least appeared to be silently mulling over the idea. One woman who did not seem to be listening to the conversation suddenly turned to me and said, "That is not true! Some things are permanent." I was a bit taken aback by her rather blunt exclamation, but asked her what she meant. Her response was, "I ended my marriage, and it will remain permanent."

I looked at her and gave a concessionary nod, but then I asked her to consider the following: "Yes, your divorce may be permanent, but *you* moved and became unstuck." Staring at me intently, she smiled begrudgingly and nodded in agreement.

I invite you now to see for yourself. Take a journey with me to observe that not only our universe is in flux but every part of you is too.

Close your eyes and take a deep breath. Now imagine you are walking along a beautiful beach in the early morning of a lovely summer day. The sun is beginning to rise, and as that big red ball makes its way into the sky, a stunning masterpiece of purple, rose, and gold is developing. It is as if an artist took paint from its palette and dabbed different colors onto a canvas, about to create something new, something magnificent, something never to be seen again on this new day, this new dawn. Continuing your way along the beach, notice with each step you take, the sand is moving so slightly, and with each breath you take, oxygen is entering your body as carbon dioxide is being expelled. Perhaps now you wouldn't mind turning your attention to the water. We have a special connection to water. We are conceived in a watery substance. We need water. We are comprised mainly of water, and we are, like water, fluid. I invite you to take a journey inward, and think about the splendid design of the intricate human body. The respiratory, circulatory, muscular, and other systems are working together in synchronicity. Now imagine these systems are like the winds, strings, and brass sections of an orchestra, making beautiful harmonious music with the mighty brain conducting. What a dazzling creation! As you continue to visualize, think about the fact that every single cell of every part of your internal workings are in motion. Lavish movement truly abounds. Now just take a moment and enjoy the internal rhythms and fluidity of you. Whenever you are ready, take another breath and slowly open your eyes. Notice how you feel. Allow yourself a few moments to savor this experience.

When I have used this visualization with clients, they have expressed pleasure around embarking on such a tranquil excursion. When we finish, some have indicated their wish for it to never end. They smile when I remind them that even good things sometimes must end, another example of inconstancy. They know, however, they can close their eyes, focus, and evoke the image at any time.

My purpose for suggesting this exercise was for you to get in touch with movement. With all this external and internal fluidity, we know people get stuck personally and professionally. Consequences can be innumerable. When it is personal, the impact may have a ripple effect on all areas of life. If it is professional, not only may it create job insecurity and alienation of coworkers, but it can also affect family relationships and friendships. When this circuitous pattern occurs, stagnation seems to prevail, and the world begins to feel very dark, ugly and negative. Even during such stuck and stark periods, movement prevails, and, with that, beauty and light still exist.

CHAPTER 3

Get Unstuck: Look for the Collateral Beauty

Not long ago, I reluctantly went to see the movie *Collateral Beauty* starring the fabulous Will Smith, Helen Mirren, and Edward Norton. My hesitation to attend was based on the trailers I had seen and mixed reviews I had read. Well, it was most fortuitous I ignored my impressions from both. The movie had a great impact on me. It was sad but haunting, and the phrase "look for the collateral beauty" resonated with me. Now let me be clear: The theme, the death of a child, is incomprehensible to imagine, and it is difficult to find meaning and beauty when such a tragedy occurs. If you look at the message on a broader scale, looking for collateral beauty is essential to survive in a world which can be quite unpredictable. What choice do we have? Sadly, and, at times, understandingly, some are unable to find it. Others, however, recognize they must search for collateral beauty as a way to become unstuck and find meaning, even after the unspeakable occurs. Somehow, they begin to move in a different direction and seek beauty by engaging in charitable acts of goodwill and kindness. Although nothing can ever completely ease the deep wounds tragedy inflicts, such meaningful actions can assuage some of the pain and allow the light to emit again.

Light always finds a way to permeate the darkness. I have a lovely cousin who is losing her vision. As her eyesight diminishes, her light sensitivity increases, and her eyes actually blister when they're exposed to the light. This wonderful person has searched for every contraption to stop the light from entering her visual range. Thus far, she has been unable to do so. No matter what she attempts regarding eyewear and other accessories, the light filters through. Although it is a painful metaphor, her situation reminds us that light penetrates the darkest of barriers. In addition, my cousin maintains a sunny disposition even as her eyesight withers. Her humor, effervescence, and belief in possibilities help her cope with the loss and the pain of her affliction. Without ignoring the sadness she expresses from time to time, she always finds a way to look for beauty under the most arduous of circumstances. I remind her that her attitude toward life and its shortcomings is a beam of light wherever she goes.

Although some people's circumstances may not be as dire as my cousin's, none of us will escape life's unfair challenges. In fact, we will receive wounds, and their eventual scar tissue, or what I refer to as the "splinters in the heart." Hopefully, we heal, accept life's battles, and continue to develop tools to prevent futility and atrophy. Also, we must savor those intermittent periods of peace and joy and allow them to embed in our brain. By doing so, we can draw upon them when collateral beauty and light are difficult to find.

Searching for beauty and light is not always visual, as my visually impaired cousin can attest and exemplify.

How about sounds such as laughter? What a beautiful gift from the universe! Laughter allows us to experience collateral beauty by lightening the mood. Not only does it move us physically and emotionally, but laughter is also infectious and engaging. Think about a time when you saw someone laughing or they told you a story which made you laugh. Maybe tears were streaming down your face. What fun you were having!

Take a moment now, close your eyes, and think of that image or a similar one which made you laugh so much you could not stop for several seconds. Really immerse yourself in the scene. Notice the smile it puts on your face. Recognize it as a testament to the fact that things can shift quickly. For many, laughter is curative; it is evidence that becoming unstuck may not be an insurmountable feat. Not only does it change your mood, but maybe, just maybe, a positive or creative thought will enter your mind which can alter the course of your direction. Voila! The collateral beauty has begun to reveal itself, and it is just the beginning.

Another sound that creates collateral beauty is music. Some music is fast and allows us to move and feel excited, free, and lighthearted. Even people who do not enjoy dancing or appear to be stoic and stiff cannot help but sway their body when the rhythm touches their spirit. A great example of this is in the movie *Genius*, a story about the friendship between renowned book editor Max Perkins and the literary giant Thomas Wolfe. In one scene, the serious and subdued Mr. Perkins, played by Colin Firth, is at a nightclub with the colorful Mr. Wolf, reenacted by Jude Law. The music is jazzy and bluesy, and Mr. Wolfe is having the time of his life. Mr. Perkins, in his somberness, slowly begins to smile and tap his foot. The rhythm and sensuality of this kind of music cannot help touch even the most restrained.

Even people who do not dance can become mesmerized by the beautiful fluidity of dance. Look at the popularity of T.V. shows like *Dancing With The Stars* and *So You Think You Can Dance*. One of my favorite dances to observe is the Argentine Tango. Watching the footwork of the experienced Tango partners is magical. How about watching a belly dancer? Recently, a few of my high school friends and I attended a classmate's show at an assisted living facility. She and her troupe were performing a variety of Middle Eastern dances. Being half Lebanese, it was a treat for me to watch and be reminded of my heritage and family. Some of the dances were familiar, but there were a few which were not, including an Egyptian cane dance. As I looked around the room, I saw a number of older adults moving and clapping to the music. As they took in the beauty of these ancient dances, they appeared to be enchanted and moved. Watching these majestic women dance was captivating. They were all ages and sizes. You could see in their dance they were experiencing beauty through the marriage of music and movement, and we were the recipients of the collateral beauty.

Other music creates deep movement within, allowing us to experience collateral beauty in another form. Classical music generates this for me. When listening, I experience beauty and light on many levels and find tears rolling down my face because of the raw emotion it evokes. Recently, I became reacquainted with the classical guitar. I forgot how much I enjoyed the beauty of this tantalizing music.

Music is so powerful and can transform us. I am sure you agree! What is your favorite music? Again, close your eyes and imagine it. Better yet, if you have it readily available, go ahead and play it! See how much you will move or be moved, or maybe both! If nothing else, it proves the fact that if you can move; you can get unstuck!

Collateral beauty is everywhere, and it is not just revealed through images and sound. How about through smell and touch? Why do you think aroma-therapy is so popular? How about all the women and men who wear a favorite cologne which is often the final embellishment for feeling beautiful? What about hugging and holding another human being, a loved partner/spouse, beloved pet, and most precious for many, a miraculous child? How about massages and spa treatments which mix touch and scent?

Collateral beauty can be experienced on many levels. Because we are so visual, we often forget about the expression of our other senses. We will discuss the importance of the multisensory experience as a skill in a later chapter. For now, as Helen Mirren aptly stated in the movie, "Look for the collateral beauty." As you do, watch what happens on your journey to becoming unstuck.

CHAPTER 4

Get Unstuck: Habits = Behavior That Can Change

In 2013, Gallup did a national survey about the state of affairs in the American workplace. Disturbingly, they discovered that 70 percent of workers are dissatisfied with their jobs. Of that 70 percent, 18 percent were found to be highly disengaged, and, consequently, undermined their coworkers and companies. In the past, corporate America has tried different approaches to ameliorate workplace unhappiness. They scheduled lunch gatherings, purchased ping-pong tables, and pursued other perks to boost morale and increase motivation. These attempts were short term, and, although well intentioned, they ended up being costly and ineffective. Conclusively, Gallup determined that the American worker's satisfaction would improve if their manager or supervisor acknowledged their strengths and took a more positive approach in their interactions with their subordinates. In addition, Gallup hypothesized that if corporate America applied this method that American productivity would double. Ultimately, profitability would increase, and everyone would benefit, from worker to corporation to shareholder to the economy. As we can see, this is major, and it points to the importance of using a positive message to help people get unstuck. The benefits of a positive approach are not surprising for those of us in the helping profession.

Even with the results of the survey, many work cultures continue to be negative, which can have negative effects on all aspects of a worker's life. Excuses are often made for those talented managers who were promoted for their work rather than their people skills. Their negative behavior is frequently ignored. They are visionaries, some might say, or they are good at their craft. Others say, "this is just the way he or she is, so just ignore them," or "don't take it personally." Many people are convinced that people do not change or are not capable of altering their behavior. As someone who has been in the people business for over 30 years, I see this as a defeatist position. In fact, everyone, in my humble but experienced opinion, is capable of change, because as my visualization displays, it is occurring within us and all around us. We are not talking about personality. This discussion is about changing behavior, because when we change our behaviors we become unstuck and open to the possibilities.

Before we discuss wrong attitudes around changing behavior, let us look more closely at the impact of this study. Why? It is a universal theme and has a bearing on all our relationships. When a parent asks an adolescent to tidy their room, instead of focusing on what is not done, they should point out their successes. At the end, the parent can mention that next time they could do such and such. Now this may be a simplistic approach, but it can be applied in the home with children and spouses and in the workplace with subordinates.

Let me give you an example of my own. Many years ago, there was a movie called *Sleepless in Seattle* which some of you probably remember. I will never forget the scene between Rob Reiner and Tom Hanks where Mr. Reiner was complaining about his wife's desire to have all the pillows on the bed. He could not comprehend her need for these decorations. I smiled because I recalled asking my husband to include all the pillows when making the bed. When he finally did this, I saw that he did not place the pillows in a way which I would have preferred, but I bit my tongue and thanked him anyway. At a later date, I asked him to consider placing them in a different fashion. All of us need to be acknowledged for our attempts and strengths because doing so will motivate a person further. In my role as therapist, I had to understand a client's pathology and vulnerabilities. To a varying degree, every human being has faults, but our strengths are what heal us and help us get unstuck. By focusing on the positive traits of others, we will see far greater improvement.

Words are like fine surgery, as a graduate school supervisor told me long ago. I could not agree more. When I, like many others, suggest focusing on the positive, it does not mean that people should be praised for nothing nor should they be coddled. In fact, their behavior needs to be addressed if they are not performing well personally or professionally. Our overly indulgent society is in danger of lowering the bar too much and decreasing expectations. Such an approach not only lacks effectiveness, but it can create more harm than good. We must always raise the bar and expect more from ourselves and others. The way it is executed, however, is the issue here.

When I was a first-term senior in high school, my average in Anatomy and Physiology was 89.75. The teacher had the choice of rewarding me with an A- or a B+. He decided to give me the lesser grade. On Parents' Night, my mother asked him the reason for his choice. He looked at her, smiled, and said, "Because she can do better." When my mother told me, we saw it as a compliment; later that year, I worked more diligently and received the coveted A. His confident message prompted me toward higher aspirations. He could have said, "She did not deserve it." Maybe I would have still worked harder, being a devoted student, but the negative approach would have been far less encouraging. The bottom line is:

Why not go with the positive stance? The chances are much more likely to reap greater rewards and assist some in getting unstuck.

Changing behavior involves changing a habit. What is a habit? According to *Merriam-Webster*, a habit is a pattern of behavior which is acquired due to repetition and becomes regular. Habits begin in the conscious and eventually become unconscious. Can habits be changed? Yes, but they are stubborn and difficult to alter. Like any success, it takes work and determination. If someone is ready to become unstuck from an unhealthy habit or behavior, they can and will do it. As the great Napoleon Hill stated: "Whatever the mind can conceive and believe, it can achieve." When I heard this quote, not long ago, I became enchanted with it because it speaks to the core of my belief system. There is no doubt in my mind that everyone, if they choose, can become unstuck, even from the most tenacious habits or behaviors. In fact, I believe we have this ability throughout our lives, which affords us the opportunity to explore new areas of productivity or unchartered territories of creativity.

In 2015, I wrote a blog post about this and was chastised. A few people emphatically expressed to me that I was wrong and by a certain age we must come to terms with just *being*. Well, I am not quite sure what they meant by "just being" and am not certain they themselves understood the meaning of their position. Certainly, it is their choice to live the remainder of their lives as they see fit. My firm stance, however, is that all of us should remain productive, creative, or find meaning to remain unstuck. Otherwise, people are missing an opportunity to bring greater fulfillment, even toward the last chapter of their lives. As Rabbi Kushner mentioned in his thought-provoking book, *Overcoming Life's Disappointments*, sometimes the best part of the game is the last few innings.

Before I discuss the science behind lifelong movement, let me give examples to refute the idea that people are incapable of change as they age. What about the fact that people take up new hobbies or develop new skills after age 50? Look at all the people who begin new careers. The writer Dominick Dunne's professional identity as a producer in Hollywood was finished when he began his career as an investigative journalist and author which was prompted by his beloved daughter's tragic death. The Canadian author Carol Shields also began writing seriously after age 50. How about the artist Grandma Moses who did not begin painting in earnest until her late seventies? I say, "You go girl." President George W. Bush pursued a painting career after he left office and was over 60. What about the writer Harry Bernstein whose first book was published when he was 96? Yes, that is correct, age 96. Before their creative sparks took off, these people were not so extraordinary. You might say that they are the exception. We do not know because they ignored their age as a limitation and pursued those untapped talents which had remained dormant for years. You and I are not any different. It is about choice. If one's goals are less lofty, think about the fact that so many people develop a new skill or hobby in their later years. Some begin to learn a musical instrument. Others participate in games such as golf and bridge. There are even a few who go out to learn a foreign language. Perhaps there is an inner artist, writer, founder, or discoverer in you? As evidenced by these aforementioned luminaries, you *can* teach an old dog new tricks. You could be one of them if you choose to and stay the course.

Now let us return to the everyday behavior of the young and old. In my role as a hypnotherapist, I have witnessed people eliminating phobias as well as unhealthy habits such as nail biting, smoking, overeating, and other behaviors which have interfered in living healthier, more fulfilling lives. Yet, people often make excuses for behavior which impedes relationships. Some will say, "Oh, they have ADD or OCD or a touch of Asperger's." I am not dismissive of those burdens which can cause much suffering. They are certainly liabilities, but how does it benefit anyone to just focus on the pathology (which our 21st century society is exceptional at doing)? Consequently, our lowered expectations may prevent true talent from awakening.

Recently, I worked with a lovely woman whose young son has difficulty communicating. Rather than excuse his behavior, she helps him develop the skills which do not come naturally to him. He had to ask a few people some questions with her guiding him. She started out by asking him to just look at their faces. This devoted mother knows that communication skills are important for her son to live a healthier, more balanced life. Our era of texting and emailing makes it easier to allow for certain behavioral styles, but in the long run, to overcome these budding impediments helps contribute to growth.

We must continue to be open to the *probability* that every human being has an ability to excel. I do not have to justify this statement because the innovation of the last century proves it. Our lives have become easier, safer, and freer as a result of humanity's evolving talent. Without being a Pollyanna, can you imagine how much humanity would benefit if everyone had the ability to explore their unique gifts? Maybe someday, but in the meantime, anyone who wishes to become unstuck must recognize their ability to become so. If you doubt me, think about that exercise I suggested earlier and go inward to connect with the movement all around you. Now get ready to hear about the science that substantiates everything I am discussing. It will prepare you for the tools and reminders I have in store for you.

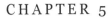

CHAPTER 5

Get Unstuck: The Blessing of Neuroplasticity

Many of you have heard of this remarkable science referred to as neuroplasticity, but I think it is important to review it as it relates to getting unstuck. I learned about neuroplasticity in Dr. Norman Doidge's book, *The Brain That Changes Itself*, and was thrilled by the potential our malleable brain has to offer. What exactly is neuroplasticity? It is the ability of the brain to change itself through thought and activity. As much as there are positive outcomes, some negativity can also emerge, because once a change is made, difficulty arises in eradicating it. I won't spend time discussing the negative outcomes, but remember our discussion earlier. Both constructive and destructive habits start in the conscious and become embedded in the unconscious. For our discussion, the belief is that the negative can be decreased or replaced with the positive.

Neuroplasticity appears to have infinite implications for humanity. For many centuries, scientists believed that the brain was like a machine. Once a part broke, repair was virtually impossible. In the earlier part of the 20th century, scientists challenged this belief as they performed more experiments. They began to accept that children had brain plasticity and healing and change could occur within a certain period of time. Again, however, the belief remained that it was short-lived, and after those earlier years, the window for change closed permanently. In the 1960s, this premise was disputed. Further testing on animals revealed that plasticity occurred in the adult brain, and, most promising, that malleability is ageless! Can you imagine? Well, yes, you can, which is the point of this book.

Dr. Doidge's work brought attention to a ground-breaking idea: parts of the brain can heal with proper training and attention. How far can it go? He gives the example of an older gentleman who suffered from a disabling stroke. Through the assistance and sheer will of his beloved son, the man was able to fully function again without the lesion ever healing. Even with a devastating stroke, in many cases, the amazing brain has the ability to reorganize itself if proper time and dedication is applied.

Getting back to the imagination, I have witnessed people's ability to improve their skills through hypnosis, which is, simply put, a daydream. Over the years, I have hypnotized people to improve their performance in golf, skiing, public speaking, and test scores, among other skills. The tools lie within the individual and their desire and belief that it can happen. Neuroplasticity is evident in all aspects of this phenomenon.

There are so many examples of individuals who achieve beyond what they or anyone else believe is their potential. There are so many examples of people who defy the odds. Look at the great Isaiah Thomas, captain of the Boston Celtics. The word *superb* barely scratches the surface for how to describe him. He is only 5'8" which is almost unheard of even for a guard in professional basketball. Some might say it is because he had his famous father's assistance. Perhaps Isaiah senior guided him, but it does not matter. Without dedication, diligence, and determination, Isaiah Thomas' small stature would have stopped him from succeeding in a sport where only the vertically endowed reside.

Have you seen the film *Hacksaw Ridge*? If you answer no, I suggest you see it. The movie introduces us to a remarkable protagonist. Mel Gibson had the wisdom to share the greatness of a humble man. Many examples like this happen without us ever hearing about them. Think about people you know. As a therapist, I can think of many examples where people defeated the odds. One especially stands out. Several years ago, I saw a woman who adopted a child with severe deficits. The little girl had been sexually, physically, and emotionally abused. The damage to her appeared to be irreversible. The mother had the child tested, and her prognosis was dire. The child was thought to be mentally challenged, and because of severe deprivation, her height fell below normal limits. At the time, this decreased measurement was defined as dwarfism. The mother was not stymied by these results. In fact, the lioness within her roared, and she pursued every service available for her and her daughter. The mother's devotion paid off. Although the child continued to have deficits, new testing revealed that she was of low average intelligence rather than below. Although she was small in stature, her height was within normal limits. I will never forget this. Could the power of love change plasticity? If we take the older gentleman who recovered from a stroke because of his beloved son's dedication, and this little girl who went beyond expectations due to maternal resolve as evidence, how can it not?

Have I convinced you that you and everyone around you is capable of change? How about the fact that your change may greatly impact someone else later? You may be making a difference right this moment as you are reading this. Believe it or not, you could even be changing the course of history. This occurrence is referred to as "The Butterfly Effect." Let's talk about it next.

CHAPTER 6

Get Unstuck: The Butterfly Effect

In 1963, scientist Edward Lorenz postulated the idea that the small movements of a butterfly's wings could create tiny changes but have great impact on the other side of the world at a later time. The scientific community did not embrace this position. In fact, they were quite dubious, to say the least. As Andy Andrews points out in his beautiful rendition of *The Butterfly Effect*, a group of physicists discovered that Dr. Lorenz was correct, and yes, in fact, such a phenomenon could happen. Mr. Andrews talks further about our ability to make a difference. He gives an example of a remarkable soldier from Maine who changed the course of the Civil War and history with a singular action. If you think about it, although it can be less dramatic, all of us change the course of history through our unique acts. A few years ago, Irish author P.J. Lynch wrote a children's book about an indentured servant, John Howland, who came over on the Mayflower and went overboard. Fortunately for Mr. Howland and the rest of us, he was saved. This servant eventually married and had children. Little did he know that his life would impact the future of the United States. His descendants included the great poets Ralph Waldo Emerson and Henry Wadsworth Longfellow, as well as other accomplished Americans.

We are often unaware of the effect we have on others because we do not see the evidence until later. In fact, as the servant's story displays, we may never know the influence our actions have on another person or a later course of events. Teachers, coaches, mentors, therapists, and especially parents provide guidance, hoping for the best, but never certain of the outcome. The writer Mitch Ablom's bestseller *Tuesdays With Morrie* is based on the inspiration he received from his dying professor with whom he reconnected long after graduating from college. Sometimes, a single word, sentence, or conversation resonates for a lifetime, as exemplified in Mr. Ablom's book. Think about who may have influenced you through their kind words or actions. Although negativity may leave a searing wound, acts of love and kindness help us heal and reveal the goodness in humanity.

If you are parents, you may be surprised by how much your children listen to you, even when you feel they are not. Often, teachers have no idea of the effect they have on their students. Sometimes they learn later in life, or maybe it is brought to light long after they leave this world. When the actor Al Pacino received his Academy Award as the disgruntled, visually impaired man in *Scent of a Woman*, he mentioned one of his teachers in his acceptance speech. One of my clients, a very dedicated teacher, told me about a parent who shared that his daughter, who is now an adult, was inspired by the teacher's passion and knowledge of literature, which contributed to her love for the subject. Prior to encountering the parent, the teacher had no idea.

We hear about coaches who motivate their teams to greatness beyond all expectations. Look at the recent Super Bowl, where the New England Patriots were expected to lose to the Atlanta Falcons. A comeback appeared to be virtually impossible, yet they did, much to the surprise and thrill of their fans. There is no doubt their drive was not only fueled by the talent and will of their quarterback, the great Tom Brady, but also because of the finesse and exceptionalism of their coach, Bill Belichick.

In my profession, I have been the receiver of the unexpected. Many years ago, when I was first doing hypnosis, a man had been referred to me for leg pain. Although I had been a psychotherapist for many years, my genesis into this evidence-based alternative treatment left me feeling a bit insecure. I saw this man three times and provided a protocol called "Glove Anesthesia." This is a technique in which the subject is taught to numb their hand and then place it to the part of the body where the pain resides. At his third and final visit, it was unclear whether this was helping alleviate the gentleman's leg pain. He decided to stop, thanked me, and did not indicate whether he gained relief from his symptoms. As a helping professional, my goal is always to help people feel better and more hopeful. Needless to say, I felt bad about the uncertain outcome of his treatment and obsessed about how it could have been better. To make matters worse, his insurance, which was supposedly offering coverage, had lapsed. I sent the client a bill assuming it would not be paid, Because I had doubts about the success of his treatment, I was not going to pursue payment. I chalked it up as a loss and did not give it much thought. A few months later, I received an envelope in the mail with a note and a check from the client. I will never forget it. In the note, he stated that he went "through hell" to get the money, but he wanted to pay me because he had experienced much relief from his symptoms. I was dumbfounded but most appreciative.

Other than teaching, no other field offers more of a window into the phenomenon of the Butterfly Effect than psychotherapy. As in the case of hypnotherapy, some forms of psychotherapy employ strategies which can be helpful. A great number of us use a variety of techniques and are eclectic, not adhering to one particular school of thought. No matter what we do, however, it is my firm belief that the importance of the relationship between the therapist and client supersedes all else, especially in longer term treatment. Psychotherapy is called a soft science and with good reason. The curative factors of the relationship are difficult to measure. The process can be ambiguous, and less does not necessarily mean more, as providers who cover these services wish to prove.

Nothing is more rewarding than helping another human being, but because growth and change does not always happen in the short term, we are often unaware if the client benefits. Once in a while, we are fortunate to find out. About ten years ago, I saw a couple for a brief time. They loved each other very much but had divergent views about having children. We met for less than five sessions, and clearly, after a brief separation, they agonized about considering the possibility of divorce. This lovely couple revealed some information as their sessions unfolded which I had failed to inquire about initially. After one extremely emotional session, they were deadlocked. They felt there was no need to continue and thanked me for my assistance. At the time, being who I am, I thought I could have been more effective in acquiring certain historical factors which may have impacted the couple's therapy. Following that fateful session, I often wondered what happened to the couple. Did they stay married? How did they reconcile their differences? Eventually, their story receded to the back shelf of my memory. Like all of us who continue to improve ourselves, I hoped I would learn from this experience.

Fast forward approximately five years later. One summer day, I was sitting in my office and perusing my mail. A package had arrived with a return address but no name. I opened it, and found a book with seemingly no notation. I smiled and wondered who sent me a book, knowing my love for books. Because there was nothing identifiable, I appreciated the surprise, but also thought I already owned this book. I assumed whoever sent it, one of my lovely clients, would eventually reveal themselves. I placed it with my carry-on, and the day proceeded without me giving it another thought as I became engrossed in my work. When I returned home and opened my briefcase, my husband saw the book and noticed a note slipping out. When I read it, I could not have been more surprised and delighted. The wife of this couple had written to me, reminding me I had lent her this book from long ago. She wanted to return it, and thank me for all I did for her and her husband. She informed me that I had a great impact on them, and they would always remember me and hold me in high esteem. Despite their strong differences, this lovely couple decided to have children and were ecstatic with the birth of their son.

I will never know what other events along their journey assisted them in this very personal decision. Perhaps they saw other therapists or one of them decided to do more work around their resistance to becoming a parent. It does not really matter. My intervention, which I judged harshly, seemed small and irrelevant at the time, yet, somehow, they saw it as having a great influence in their lives. The letter remains in my belongings, and I am forever grateful they provided me with a special glimpse into their lives of joy and contentment. If they had not, I never would have known my involvement in this Butterfly Effect.

Now allow me to share a personal decision which started a chain of events that are still unfolding in my life. In 2007, due to family health issues, my husband and I decided to leave our home of 17 years to move closer to our family and friends. We lived in Needham, Massachusetts for over 17 years, where my husband and I maintained small successful businesses. We lived five minutes from our places of business, and I had a five-minute walk from my business to my husband's place of work. By 2007, my husband had sold his original business and gave up a new one he had begun. Because I continued to maintain my practice, my husband left the decision to me whether we should make the move. For sound financial reasons as well as our need for close support, I thought we should, and we did. Other than our businesses, we were not entrenched in the Needham community, but my commute would become a 45-minute commute in heavy traffic even though it would be for only three days a week. For the last seven years, I have been driving in annoying traffic. Even though I have arranged my hours to avoid as much traffic as possible, it is still quite tiring at this time in my life. When I question the decision,

I review the fortuitous events which would not have occurred had we not moved, and I conclude that this is an example of the Butterfly Effect at its best. Let me elucidate.

When I left Needham, I thought about establishing a private practice in central Massachusetts, which I tried twice. The first time, I did it as a solo practitioner, and even though I began to see lovely clients, I found it to be far too isolating and subsequently closed the office. The second time around, I considered joining a group practice, which I believed emulated the one of which I was a partner for over 18 years. I even gave notice to my Needham practice which I submitted to the Executive Committee. Within a short time, however, I rescinded after recognizing that as successful as the new practice appeared to be, it was not the same as my unique business in Needham.

Although I was relieved with my decision, I remained restless about spending the rest of my career solely as a therapist. I adored my clients and loved helping people, but I knew there was something else beckoning me. My beloved mother's one-way flight to Heaven in February 2015 intensified my desire for something more in this next chapter of my life. After much contemplation, an idea began to germinate. I had spoken a couple of times about my unique private practice, and I was quite comfortable speaking from a platform. I began writing and posting blogs on the rudimentary website I developed as well as on LinkedIn, trying to promote my speaking business but not having other tools to further my ambition. I felt passionate about my subject matter, and I knew I would be passionate and engaging on stage. The issue for me was narrowing my message and determining what and to whom I was going to speak.

During the summer of 2015, I spent some time on LinkedIn where I learned of an Intuitive named Lynne Robinson. From everything I read, she seemed quite credible and had a stellar background so I set up a half-hour consult with her. My conversation with Ms. Robinson led me on an inspirational path of no return. In our discussion, I shared with Ms. Robinson some of my thoughts. She suggested I explore the National Speakers Association, a group of which I had not been familiar. Ms. Robinson seemed quite knowledgeable about this group, and everything I was hearing reverberated with everything I desired. After researching this group, I attended the New England Chapter's first event following the summer recess. It was an auction event, and I bid on a woman who had expertise in the service of marketing and strategy. Her name was Marilee Driscoll. That same day, I decided to join as an academy member because I wanted to devour the knowledge and training they offered.

The same month I joined NSA, a new friend of mine who happened to view me on LinkedIn encouraged me to consider a visit to Toastmasters. At that time, I had an image of Toastmasters as a group of people who spontaneously alternated speaking because of their fear of public speaking. Later it became clear that my knowledge about this remarkable organization was truly limited. In fact, I canceled the first visit to my friend's club, and when I finally decided to attend, I did so begrudgingly. My arrival on that early September Thursday changed my life forever. I listened to the various speakers and decided to join on the spot. As you can see, it does not take me long to decide. Toastmasters incorporates my narrow version, but it is so much more. In fact, as many people have stated, it is one of the best kept secrets about lifelong learning. If you are someone who wishes to get unstuck, Toastmasters may be the genesis of that solution. Not only is it about speaking, but equally important, it assists you in improving the understated sibling, listening. I will talk more about the importance of listening when we begin to explore the use of my D.R.E.A.M. technique.

Since becoming a member of NSA and Toastmasters, my quest toward becoming a professional speaker as well increasing my writing has exploded. I joined a Fast Track program for beginning speakers and am on my journey of acquiring the coveted 20 speeches to receive professional membership with the National Speakers Association which has already taken place at this reading. With Toastmasters, I have achieved the first two awards in communication as well as the first in leadership and have been awarded the Triple Crown. For me, achieving and pursuing is an ongoing process, and when I feel a bit stuck, I remind myself of the significance of setting goals toward greater accomplishment.

In addition, Marilee, my savvy strategy coach, not only has assisted me in discovering my theme of "Unstuck," but she introduced me to Napoleon Hill as well as motivating me to write a newsletter. Both actions contributed toward my attainment of the next desired chapter in my life. Let me further explain.

Until 2016, I had never heard of Napoleon Hill, and I am not alone, at least among mental/behavioral health specialists. After reading his book, *Think and Grow Rich*, I fell in love with Dr. Hill's philosophy of success, which seems to integrate some elements of positive psychology. Every time I query a mental health or educational professional about Napoleon Hill, they look at me dumbfounded, and I share that I was equally uninformed about this stranger in our professional world until I read his books. Oh, how deprived we have been...Napoleon Hill was prescient! In addition to positive psychology, his universal theme embodies the use of autosuggestion which I believe is related to the use of hypnotic suggestion. As I absorbed his eloquent messages, I thought more about my purpose and it propelled me further toward my newfound goals of writing and speaking.

After reading Dr. Hill's books, I saw something on Facebook about a movie being produced which was based on *Think and Grow Rich*. I linked to the information and made a very small donation toward this anticipated project. Within a few months, I received another book from the Napoleon Hill Foundation. I had never heard of his foundation, but I researched it. I devoured the gift I received, a further discussion of his principles. Eventually another book arrived.

At about the same time that I was learning more about Dr. Hill, I began writing a newsletter and acquiring email addresses. I reached out to some of my contacts, and asked if I might share my "short and sweet" newsletter with them. One of the people was the congenial administrator from a publishing company with whom I had come in contact. Like many others she was quite receptive, and I thought nothing more about it. After reading one or two of the newsletters which included a blog, she apparently went to my website and read some of my other blogs. Subsequently, she contacted me and asked if wouldn't mind her sharing my written material with the publisher. She reminded me there were no guarantees but thought it made sense to at least present the information. I responded with gratitude and let her know I understood the risk. The proverb of "nothing ventured, nothing gained" certainly bears merit, and, as far as I was concerned, to reach his attention was an honor. Fortuitously, the publisher read some of my blogs and expressed interest in further communication. After an email exchange, we scheduled a phone call. We talked a day before my new video event, and it was a very pleasant and promising exchange. I gave the publisher a synopsis of the message in my keynote, and he informed me that I could use much of it for my book. In addition, when I told him of one of the statements I use in the keynote as well as with many of my clients, "Stop Depriving the World of You," he suggested that as a title. As you can see, I concurred. What did that conversation do for me? It catapulted me into doing even more. I wrote more newsletters and began writing my book as well, vigorously marketing myself to book more of those beginning speeches.

When I shared my belief that our residential move created this chain of events which I view as my Butterfly Effect, some people minimized it. Their response was that I was ready and open for it. They are correct to the extent that I could have chosen to ignore all the delicious openings and offerings. My belief, however, is that without that momentous move I would not have followed the magnificent road I find myself traversing. Other than the stagnant reimbursement from insurance companies, I was somewhat content working four days a week five minutes from home and continuing my goal of acquiring more private pay clients through my experience as a hypnotherapist. The move to central Massachusetts added more stress because of the commute, yet it gave me an extra day to ponder about the future and my upcoming years as a psychotherapist. When I asked my husband his opinion regarding the impact of the change, he agreed with me wholeheartedly. I am convinced that I would not have arrived where I am if the move had not occurred.

Take a moment and close your eyes. Imagine the beautiful butterfly, elegantly fluttering by as it moves its wings. Now, visualize a change on the other side of the world. The actions may be connected. Close your eyes again and take a deep breath and let it out! Begin to think about your own Butterfly Effect. Many unfold during our lifetimes, but some are far more consequential than others. Maybe a significant one occurred, and you ignored the ripple effects of its impact. Conceivably, the important event may not have revealed itself at this time. Be on the lookout, because you do not know when it will take place. More notably, be open, because you may not recognize the vastness of the impact until later. As the story I shared illustrates, small movements or not-so-easy transitions can render a powerful movement at a later point. Such movement can help one embrace more fulfilling change as it has for me, or it can help one become unstuck as it has done and will continue to do so for many people. How lovely it is to see that none of us needs to remain stuck; if you choose, the scrumptious possibilities are ripe for your picking.

CHAPTER 7

The "U" in Unstuck

Like many speakers and writers, I love acronyms and am pleased the letters in the word *unstuck* can be used to add more words that represent being unstuck. Let us start with "U," the first letter in *unique.* How apropos to our discussion of getting unstuck! Why? Because it is your uniqueness which will help you become unstuck, and you are most unique. There is absolutely no one else like you. Just like the brilliant stars in the sky, the sparkling diamonds, the marvelous trees, you are one of a kind. Think for a moment how splendid that is! Even identical twins who may share the same DNA, have a unique set of fingerprints, as well as a unique conscience and soul. No matter how much one tries to be like another human being, it can't be done.

Why would anyone *want* to be like someone else? I do not understand it. We often hear that people wish to be another Oprah, Tom Brady or Gisele Bundchen. They may have attributes we admire, but to try to emulate one of these people means you are stuck! Why not focus on being the improved, unique you? Trying to copycat another person deprives you of discovering your own unique talents and gifts. Some gifts are dormant, waiting to be awakened. Why not begin to explore what is submerged? You might say that you are not talented or have unique gifts. How do you know if you don't try? Please do not give me the, "It is too late," or "I am too old." If you have read this far, you know I will counter such limiting responses with what I wrote earlier. Those extraordinary people who discovered their own flair at various times in their lives are not any different than you when it comes to being unique. Yes, they are unique and so are you. They are exceptional because they chose to use their uniqueness by tapping into their hidden talents. Not only that, but they invited their talents to come forth and looked steadily for the wave that pushed them over any barriers in their path. Their uniqueness shined through, just as yours can too.

Now perhaps you wouldn't mind closing your eyes and allowing yourself to go to a place of beauty. Begin to think about yourself in this wondrous setting and focus on your uniqueness. Allow words to emerge. When you have allowed this to happen, open your eyes and take a pen and paper or maybe some colored markers and begin to write about your uniqueness, not just your outer appearance, but your inner characteristics. Do you have a lovely singing voice? Have you mastered the written word? Are you an artist waiting to be discovered? Are there words to describe your essence? Most noteworthy, do you listen to others and go the extra mile, something which is overlooked but a most noble quality? If your unconscious brings a few words to mind, begin to focus there.

Recently, I hypnotized a woman who did not experience herself as positively as others saw her. While she was in a state of wellbeing, I used the language she offered to me. One of the words was "rock." After suggesting she embrace the words of courage and capability which she also provided me, I verbalized "rock" by saying she was like a "rock" and "she rocked." When this lovely woman opened her eyes, she was smiling and most pleased that I had extrapolated on a word which defined her in both ways. Again, how about you? Perhaps one of those descriptions can be defined in multiple ways to provide additional meaning.

As often as possible, do the exercise I just suggested. By doing this on a regular basis, you will come to not only accept but appreciate the gift of your uniqueness. Once you do, get ready to launch!

CHAPTER 8

The "N" in Unstuck

N is for *new*. If you think about it, one moment to another is new, which is the beauty of beginning. Opportunity arises with every new sunrise, new chapter, new day. As I have shown, even the most senior of people are capable of getting unstuck and starting new. One of the most profound changes we see in fiction is from Charles Dickens' ageless classic *A Christmas Carol*. Mr. Scrooge was old, crotchety, rigid, ignorant, and stuck. Through dreams of loss and a gloomy future, old Ebenezer was able to recognize it was not too late for him. Consequently, he became unstuck and not only altered his behavior but had impact on those around him.

As much as negativity can darken and wither the spirit, creating havoc and consternation all around us, positivity can do the opposite. With a belief in being able to renew, opportunity abounds. Being able to see this newness can extricate anyone from the shackles of disappointment and loss which is unfortunately a part of life. Seeing newness does not erase our sadness, which is often severe and incomprehensible, but it offers a chance to take advantage of living. Sometimes anguish is so great it is difficult to capitalize on this, but if we want to continue to make meaning of our life on earth, we have no choice. In fact, it is not time which heals all wounds but the intervening events. They provide the salve. I learned that from a psychology professor many years ago, and I never forgot it. In fact, I tell my clients this message for which we must all be reminded.

People who remain in the past can miss the possibilities of something new. I believe there are two purposes for revisiting the past. One is to savor those delicious memories of love, celebration, and joy. Nothing stays the same, so embed in your mind those unforgettable times. These are the memories that get us through challenging times and can offer hope for better times in the future.

You might say, "How do you know it will be better?"

My answer to you would be, "We do not know, but how does it serve anyone to anticipate bleak days to come?"

Someone else could say, "Nothing ever works for me. Why hope?"

I would respond with "How do you know it won't next time?" No one knows for sure. In fact, if you continue to look at things negatively, you could miss an opportunity. Most of us have some or many memories of love or acts of kindness which we can access for hope and inspiration. Even if it is only one, you can use it to leverage your belief in getting unstuck.

The second purpose for revisiting the past is to examine what we have learned from it. In order to grow, we sometimes have to step back as a way to go forward. People often stay stuck in the past, and no matter how much they try, they cannot extricate themselves from it. That is where therapy can be helpful. A therapist can recognize the role of the past and the need for it to be explored even if only casually, in some cases. Through therapy, people can begin to understand the events which may be keeping them stuck personally and professionally. Perhaps they had a loss or troubled relationship with a parent or sibling. Trauma, which can include physical or sexual assault, may be the culprit. Obviously, there are varying degrees of impact, but whatever it may be, disturbing events often must be resurrected to put them to rest permanently. The journey is worth undertaking for those who wish to get unstuck from the ghosts of the past. With the right therapeutic partnership, release from the bondage of the past can lead to greater freedom and fulfillment than ever imagined.

Because I am a therapist/hypnotherapist/coach, I am obviously biased, but I also recognize there are many ways toward enlightenment and freedom. Some use their chosen faith to assist them. Others explore various philosophies which they believe can unbind them. I know a lovely woman who told me about the Latin American philosophy *Lagosophy* which is virtually unknown in the United States. This woman believed it to be most useful to her in how she conducted her life. While the group meetings were still available, she attended regularly and was aided in becoming unstuck from some of the past. In whatever way one embarks on their voyage, the most important feature is safety, and believing that those who are assisting you in this passage are trustworthy. You are the captain of your ship, and if you feel something is amiss with any of your crew, you have the right to tell them to disembark. Remember, part of getting unstuck from the past is taking charge of yourself and utilizing the best tools to help you do so.

Is there something new brewing in your life? Perhaps there is a new friend, relationship, or professional endeavor. If none of those appear on the horizon now, there is still newness all around you. Just look at the sunrise in the early morning or the sunset in the later evening. They are reminders that every day is new and fresh.

CHAPTER 9

The "S" in Unstuck

The letter S could be used for the beginning of so many words such as special, stellar, and splendid. All three of those words would be fitting, but I chose a word that I thought was best for our theme. *Strength* represents our ability to get unstuck. Each one of us has strengths and can exercise our mind and body for even more. Yes, some people are endowed with greater physical strength through their anatomy. I am only 4'11". The reality is, I would have difficulty overpowering a 6' man.

The mind, however, is different. Everyone is unique, but we have no limitations for exercising and strengthening our minds. As we have seen, under adversity or great challenge, many people overcome obstacles in different ways than they or anyone else thought possible. I turn again to Dr. Doidge's book *The Brain That Changes Itself.* In one chapter, he discusses the story of a political prisoner who was subjected to solitary confinement for several years. The prisoner recognized his mind would suffer from lack of stimulation and connection. Consequently, he began playing mental chess with himself. When he left prison, not only was his mind intact, but he was able to beat a world champion in the game of chess. This man's ability to think not only saved his brain cells but made him stronger. Many people are so diligent with exercising their body for strength and health, yet they take the magnificent human mind for granted. The mind orchestrates the body, and it needs to be nurtured for sustenance and strength.

Begin to think about the unique strengths which describe you. Do not underestimate any of them! You may see yourself as a rock, as my lovely client described, or maybe you "rock" as I suggested to her. It does not matter if you use similar language as someone else. Because of your uniqueness, your strengths will be uniquely experienced and displayed.

Begin to write a few words to characterize your strengths. Reflect on them. Next, look in a mirror and say the words out loud. Give it a try and then repeat it. If you initially feel awkward, it will pass. As you are doing the exercise a third time, examine your body language. Put your shoulders back, hold your head high, and allow yourself to smile. Notice the difference now in how you are feeling compared to before you performed this exercise. You might want to write that down. You might keep a journal, and each time you recite your strengths, jot a few thoughts down or even just one word of the experience. Consider making a ritual of this and watch what happens. Eventually, a feeling of empowerment will flow throughout your being. In addition, when you keep your unique strengths front and center, you are reminded they are present during good and not-so-good times.

Let me now suggest a few visualizations which I have created or modified. In addition to writing, tapping into the right side of our brain can be invaluable. We see our ability to use our splendid and unlimited imagination. Here are three exercises:

Tapestry of Life

Close your eyes and imagine a beautiful tapestry made of gorgeous jewels. As you examine it, you see the buoyant colors of youth: the jewels of pink tourmaline, aquamarine, and blue topaz. Now look more closely. You observe amethysts and emeralds adorning it. Moving your eyes, you begin to notice a heavier section of the tapestry. You are now dazzled by the jewels of strength which you have earned along your life journey. Rubies, sapphires, and diamonds are ablaze in brilliance. Navigating the choppy waters of life, you accept that you are worthy of these glorious jewels. Now imagine cloaking yourself with this tapestry and watching it unfold and sparkle more. Feel its strength and power and imagine those feelings spreading deep into the essence of your being. You are one with the tapestry, exuding radiance and strength. As you experience the magnificence of this visual, remind yourself of all the things you have to offer. Open your eyes and write whatever comes to mind even if is just one word. You will surprise yourself.

Magnificent Warrior/Beautiful Queen

No one goes through life without being wounded. As I mentioned in my chapter on Collateral Beauty, some wounds, those splinters in the heart, are deeper than others and may feel like boulders piercing our being. That is the bad news. The better news is that you are reading this, so you have survived life's many and often unfair battles. You are now ready for this visual which I developed based on my days of participating in Yoga. I apply it on a regular basis:

Close your eyes, and imagine you are standing tall, like a magnificent Warrior or beautiful Warrior Queen. Your head is high, and your shoulders are back. You are standing in glory and splendor. Not only have you survived the battles, but you recognize your wounds are now like little laparoscopic scars. Sometimes you feel a dull ache, and some ache more than others, but they are like badges of honor. Remind yourself that you have developed even more strength and a greater will to live fully, and let yourself embrace that feeling. Now begin to experience this feeling of empowerment deep in your being, from the top of your head, out to the tips of your fingers, down to the tips of your toes. Allow yourself to bask in the glory of your empowerment, determination, and majestic presence, and let it flow deeply throughout your being.

Inner Strength

This next visual is something I modified from a hypnotic technique developed by a wonderful, brilliant physician in the field of hypnotherapy. Her name was Claire Frederick, and she was an amazing teacher. She passed away rather suddenly a couple of years ago and is sorely missed by her peers and other hypnotherapists. The technique is just lovely and can be a spectacular visual. Here it is:

Imagine that you are walking through a beautiful place. As you walk, you will begin to experience this beauty on many levels. Notice the gorgeous scene around you. Begin to listen to the glorious sounds resonating in this place of beauty. Perhaps you experience a scent or two, reminding you of how wondrous this place is. You are completely awestruck! As you continue to walk, go a little more inward and get in contact with your inner strength. Perhaps your strength is an image or a thought or a feeling. Whatever you experience, allow yourself to let this strength spread throughout your being. When you are ready to open your eyes, jot down a word of strength which immediately comes to mind. Hold onto this word, and, going forward, close your eyes and say this word on a regular basis.

If any of these three visuals connect with you, please use them. As you do, notice the difference in how you feel, even if it seems minute to you. Learn patience and build upon each step. If you do them regularly, you will notice a shift. You are exercising your mind, which is creating movement and propelling you to get unstuck. If you would like to write down these visuals, go ahead. For me, writing helps me embed suggestions in my brain. Maybe that works for you too.

If you enjoy drawing, do so with one or all of these techniques. Art is powerful, as we know. As you are writing or drawing these visuals, you may get more ideas about becoming unstuck. In addition, whether you just imagine, write, or draw, feel free to modify the visualizations according to your own needs. Maybe your tapestry will be filled with more jewels or different ones. Perhaps, your warrior or warrior queen will take on a different persona of strength. Finally, you may decide immediately or later that developing your own visuals would work best. Whatever you decide, do something, because it promotes movement and getting unstuck in the moment you begin the process. Most importantly, remember that the use of visuals and how you imagine them will be unique because of your own uniqueness.

Before moving onto the next letter, I just want to say something about imagination and the other senses. We, the products of the 20th and 21st century, are visual beings. We rely heavily on our eyes. In past centuries, however, people focused on the use of other senses, as Carolyn Purnell writes in her delightful book, *The Sensational Past*. The book discusses an emphasis on senses other than sight, especially during and after the Enlightenment. As someone who often has people imagine an experience on a multi-sensory level, the book is a fascinating read. Think about it! Sometimes memories are evoked through sound, smell, touch, and taste, which is why we draw on some of our other senses to augment our visuals.

CHAPTER 10

The "T" in Unstuck

Did you enjoy Greek and Roman Mythology? My favorite is the story of Cupid and Psyche, an enchanting myth about love, jealousy, and immortality. Psyche means soul, and perhaps the universe drew me to this myth because I ended up in a field, Psychology, which was originally defined as the study of the soul.

Some of the myths are not so pleasant, such as the myth of Sisyphus. According to mythology, Sisyphus committed crimes and was condemned for eternity to roll a heavy ball up a hill and watch it roll back down over and over. Thankfully, his plight is mythical, but doesn't that myth generate a feeling of déjà vu? I suspect there are times that all of us feel like

Sisyphus. During those frustrating episodes, it feels like that ball keeps rolling down, no matter how much effort we put into pushing it over the hill. Our tenacity is tested, which is the reason I chose *tenacious* to represent the letter "T" in unstuck. Although there are times we feel like Sisyphus, we are *not* Sisyphus. Every one of us has the ability to push the ball over the hill, but only those who are tenacious will succeed.

Tenacity, also known as grit, is often the singular characteristic of the most successful people in the world. Frequently, they are lackluster students, and their intelligence, creativity, and talent do not appear exceptional. In fact, all of us hear stories about the unassuming person who surprises everyone with their unexpected rise to great success. Some of these people seemed destined for mediocrity.

Some of the visuals I suggested in the last chapter can help you not only recognize your unique strengths but also develop your tenacity. Sometimes our greatest challenge is to not succumb to defeat. All of us endure failure, yet we have a choice. Either we give up, shut up, or we get up and keep going. Anyone who has been my client knows my response when they express frustration about their seemingly futile efforts. They are gently but firmly reminded they must continue. Perhaps there is a different approach, but surrender is not an option. Often, I share my own stories to show that I practice what I preach. Here is one:

During my first year of graduate school, I was an insecure, sheltered young woman. I had a field advisor, Ms. M., who for some reason frightened me. She was older and did not exude much warmth. At the beginning of the year, Ms. M. gave us a non-graded essay to write. When I met with her, as all her assigned students were required, Ms. M. forebodingly informed me that my writing was sub-par and it would require much diligence for me to succeed in my graduate studies. Needless to say, I was devastated, but I was determined to improve my situation. That weekend, I went to the library and began scrupulously writing my first assignment for a class entitled Human Behavior. The paper was about dissecting the boundaries of a dysfunctional family and highlighting a particular member of your choosing. While I was writing, I ran into a classmate, Barbara Lieberman, who became a fast and steady friend. I told her my plight with Ms. M., also her field advisor. Barbara looked at my written work and indicated she saw no problems with my writing. She made one suggestion and told me I would do well. I completed the paper and was pleased with the final piece. After submitting it to the professor, I said a prayer and just reminded myself I did the best I could do. A week later, the papers were returned to us and graded with a V, V- or V+. When she handed me my graded essay, I closed my eyes for a moment. When I opened them, I was overjoyed. The professor had written V++++ and said it was one of the best written papers she had seen. My ebullience could not be put into words. I decided to make a visit to Ms. M. so I could express my gratitude for her feedback. At that moment, I believed her pessimism had pushed me to work ferociously at changing the narrative. When I expressed my appreciation and also honestly let her know I had been mistakenly intimidated by her, Ms. M. proceeded to inform me that she too had erred. Ms. M. confused me with another student who had the letter C for her last name and was similarly small in stature. Ms. M. indicated my writing had been just fine. When Ms. M. divulged this, I was a bit taken aback, but believed her inaccuracy helped me to develop greater tenacity.

This field advisor went on to challenge me again later in the year regarding my clinical skills. In fact, this was much more damaging to my psyche. Why? I was so committed to becoming a helping professional that I could not allow anything to derail it. In between semesters I contracted the flu, and, upon my return, my immediate supervisor told me she thought I might not return. That had never crossed my mind. What the feedback did was to energize me to work even harder. That second semester I pursued anything and everything to hone my clinical skills. I wanted to understand the process, which was like learning a foreign language. I participated in my own therapy because of this crisis, and finally that spring, while sitting with a very sad and abused young woman, it clicked. *Ah*, I said to myself, *this is what they mean by process.* Tenacity prevailed, and I went on to the next year with much more confidence.

Not long after my experience with Ms. M., I discovered she was extremely brutal to other students who were older and more experienced than me. Even more validation came a few years later when I attended a national conference for social workers. One of the presenters talked about the ludicrousness of the first-year experience. With much humor, he prompted us to recall how they threw us into a situation and expected us to magically comprehend the process. I sat there feeling so vindicated, realizing I had not been alone in my experience. As I reflected, I knew if I had been overly sensitive and without tenacity, I would not have prevailed.

How has tenacity helped you overcome what Sisyphus could not? Are there times you gave up? If so, you know what? So what! If you are dwelling on past failures or are mired in regret, you are stuck. Been there, done that, and tell yourself firmly *not again*. Think about the letter "N" for new and use your uniqueness, strengths, and tenacity to start anew. If you think it will help you, write a goodbye letter to the regret or lost opportunity. Often it can be a therapeutic exercise to finally let things go. Give it a try and watch what happens.

CHAPTER 11

The "U" in Unstuck

We are back to the letter "U" again. We are going to repeat the word *unique* because by now you must be thinking about some of your unique attributes. Perhaps you were able to write a few words about your uniqueness. Again, they may be the same words used by others, but applying them to your own uniqueness makes them automatically unique. Are you truly on board with understanding your ability to get unstuck? Have you started to think about the collateral beauty surrounding you? Do you believe you can change your habits and behaviors? How about the Butterfly Effect? Has it manifested in a way so that you can connect the dots between one event and another? Maybe one event has happened but the other has not yet occurred or revealed its true impact. Have you begun to regularly contemplate how everything is new and how exciting that is? Even if you are advancing in years, the fact you remain on this earth gives you a chance to explore something new. Are you able to visualize your strengths through the suggestions I made or your own? Yes, all these questions should be answered in a way which is unique to you. I encourage you to celebrate your uniqueness. If anyone in your life sends the message that you are nothing special, I encourage you to hold tight to your uniqueness. In fact, I will give you a sentence I frequently use to reinforce your sense of uniqueness: The unique you is worthy and deserving of feeling good. You will not let anything or anyone interfere with this. You are on your way to feeling happier and healthier and more freed up than in ways you may never have thought possible.

Celebrate your uniqueness! Discover what lies within you! Your talents and gift are emerging as you read this. Now it is time to be creative and utilize them.

CHAPTER 12

The "C" in Unstuck

How divine is it to have "C" be the next letter of Unstuck? The word *creativity* could not be more appealing for the letter C. Creativity is part of our essence. First and foremost, we, human beings, are blessed to be a most exquisite creation. No matter how you believe our species began, it is evident that we are a complex design of epic proportions. There are many fascinating unfoldings in our universe, but nothing can match the intricacy, uniqueness, and marvel of the human being. In addition, we are given a great mind which can create. When people think about creativity, they assume people are gifted in the arts, music, writing, and innovation. Some people tapped into their gifts in their youth. For others, talents are often dormant waiting to be awakened at a later stage in life. How about expanding the notion of creativity? Let us begin.

First of all, those of you who are parents created another unique human being which makes you the greatest of creators. Think about the majesty of this creation! Several swimming sperm compete to reach a single egg or two within a certain period of time within another small window of time. It is quite a challenge, yet it has been occurring since the dawn of humankind, over and over. The process itself is something to marvel, but the beauty of the final product cannot be put into words. The winning sperm and egg combine the DNA of both partners to create something simply magnificent. Need I say more?

Creativity reveals itself in ways we take for granted as it is embodied in many professions. The old saying, "It is the singer not the song" has great meaning. The most effective teachers are creative in their use of self to capture students' attention even for the most desultory of subjects. Along with teaching, this talent is imparted in the world of mental health. Often one must be authentically creative to engage people unfamiliar or distrustful of the psychotherapy process. As speakers, we must use our creativity to influence the audience in the hope they depart with something you evoked in them.

There are so many ways that creativity is a part of everyday life. I once had a supervisor who said, "Words are like fine surgery." That creative statement has stayed with me for over 35 years, and I believe by creatively altering words in a sentence, we can have great impact on another human being.

Now go ahead and write down ways you have been creative. Please do not say you have not. If you have used any of the visuals I suggested, you are creating even if they are a script I suggested. The visualization is unique and yours. You have created it!

CHAPTER 13

The "K" in Unstuck

I am a bibliophile. All right, let me be honest. Stated more bluntly, I am a bookaholic. That is correct. I adore reading. If I could be like Bradley Cooper's character in the movie *Limitless*, sans the drugs, I would so I could devour more books. My love for books is so great that I wrote a blog about it. As much as I enjoy Amazon's speedy but dangerous tool to acquire books with its one-click, I miss brick and mortar stores where you can go and touch, open and peruse. Ah, such a comfort! At this time in my life, I have so many books that I could have my own bookstore or library.

Are you wondering why I am sharing my love for books? For those of you who are less enamored with the art of reading, I suggest you at least consider some way to acquire *knowledge*, which is the word I have chosen for the letter "K" in unstuck. Knowledge is infinite, and with the internet, the greatest purveyor of information in my lifetime, you have unlimited access. Like anything else, some of the information is drivel, yet you can search and explore whatever you wish to learn.

If you are not a visual reader, the world of audio is there for your plucking. The most important message is to learn, learn, and learn. As a lifelong learner, I strongly believe everyone should continue this journey all the days of their life. Acquiring knowledge opens the mind.

Being biased, allow me to tell you my reasons for stressing books, even those which are considered light and romantic. Years ago, long before I visited San Francisco, I read some of Danielle Steele's books. That is correct, Danielle Steele, and admittedly, once in a while I still read one. Ms. Steele's books often center around the Golden Gate city, and I believe I learned a great deal about it from her books. I don't want to give the impression that every single book offers knowledge, but more do than not, even if they are cloaked in romance or fantasy.

In addition to gathering knowledge, even pleasurable reading, which is my favorite, has increased my vocabulary. Before the age of the Internet, I used to keep a dictionary next to me so I could find the definition of an unfamiliar word. I do the same now by using the Internet. Having a better vocabulary augments my speaking and writing skills, and all this stems from my voracious thirst for reading.

No matter how you acquire knowledge, never stop learning. If you want to be more successful personally and professionally, continue to access knowledge. You will always feel like you are accomplishing, and such an endeavor often allows you to share or participate in other worlds.

What have you learned lately? Do you like to read or listen? If books are not to your liking, how about learning a new skill, hobby, or language? Whatever is your pleasure, go ahead and begin. If money is a concern, the libraries continue to provide a wealth of information at no cost. If free time is an issue, take even few minutes each day and learn something new. Then, watch what happens! Even if it is a small step, it is still an achievement and will catapult you to do more.

CHAPTER 14

How to Actually Get and Stay Unstuck

As a child long before cable, I, along with other children, looked forward to the annual showing of *The Wizard of Oz*. I remember eagerly sitting in a comfortable chair on that special Sunday in April in anticipation of this enchanting, ageless spectacle. As many of us learned as we got older, the basic story had more to do with politics in the very late 1800s than captivating an audience for pure entertainment, but the magic of movies altered the message. Although the original story was a political metaphor, the movie version displayed many psychological metaphors. "If I only had a brain, heart, and courage," as Dorothy's three friends woefully expressed; the wizard ultimately provided symbols of their yearnings. Through the Good Witch of the North, Dorothy was to discover her ruby slippers carried the power to bring her home. It is not too difficult to conclude that all four of these characters yearned for something they already had embedded within their being.

Although other movies carry similar messages, this movie artfully and creatively displays the message for children and adults alike. We have the power within us to get unstuck from old messages, negative thoughts, stymied performances, inadequate communication, and unfulfilling relationships, personally and professionally. The bottom line is: You have all the basic tools and skills to get unstuck. Do they need honing? Possibly! Could you benefit from more techniques to strengthen them? Probably! Are you capable of using these tools to bring you to another level? Absolutely! Like Dorothy and her loyal friends, it is entirely up to you, and guess what? In real life, magic is genuine because it is about the power within you. Think about that potential ready to be unleashed. Are you excited yet? I hope so, and if so, you are ready to learn about a technique which I think will help you not only become unstuck but catapult you beyond your expectations. Before I introduce it, however, I am asking you do the following:

Take a piece of paper, white or a color of your choice, and fold it in half like a card. On the front, use a slim colored marker and write boldly and vertically *Unstuck* on the left side of the front. Next to each letter write the words we discussed in each chapter: U=Unique, N=New, S=Strength, T=Tenacity, U=Unique, C=Creativity, and K=Knowledge. Once you have completed this, you can open the folded paper and on the left page simply write Butterfly Effect. You do not have to write more right now. Eventually, after some contemplation, you can write an event which later contributed to changing the course of your life. As I said earlier, usually more than one will occur over a lifetime, but you may wish to think about the most momentous one. Finally, on the back page write D.R.E.A.M. perpendicularly from the left corner to the right. Voila! You are done.

Why did I suggest you do this? First, writing makes us think and is therapeutic in itself. Second, such an exercise will assist you in planting messages into your conscious and unconscious mind. Last but certainly not least, when the going gets tough, as it will, you have a visible tool to remind you of your capacity to become unstuck. Now you are ready for the D.R.E.A.M. technique.

CHAPTER 15

Dream Your Way to Getting Unstuck

Most people daydream throughout their lives. Some do it more than others. Children are the masters of daydreaming, which is the reason for their rich fantasy life. While driving, people dissociate, which is a daydream. Under hypnosis, people daydream because hypnosis is a dissociative process and, simply put, a daydream. That is correct. For many years, a number of us who are senior hypnotherapists did not phrase hypnosis in such easily-understood terms until a 90-year-old physician/hypnotherapist suggested we think of it that way. Yes, there is nothing like a daydream, because it spurs our ability to imagine the possibilities.

How about evening dreams? Did you know that famous people such as Paul McCartney, Mary Shelley,

Jack Nicklaus, and Albert Einstein, among many other luminaries, were inspired by their dreams? The incredibly gifted Mr. McCartney wrote one of the famous Beatles songs as a result of a dream. A woman ahead of her time, Mary Shelley, created the masterpiece *Frankenstein* from dreams. The talented golfer, Jack Nicklaus, believes his dreams helped him develop a new golf swing. The brilliant Albert Einstein's theory of relativity evolved from a dream. Yes, dreams do come true. Not only that, you can incubate a dream. Through hypnosis, I learned to do so from the master professor I mentioned earlier, Clair Frederick. You can learn to do it non-hypnotically as discussed by researchers including Deidre Barret, who has written several articles and a book about this phenomenon.

How about taking the idea of a dream and using it during the day? I developed this idea after years working as a therapist and a hypnotherapist. My D.R.E.A.M. technique reveals how you can actively use scripting and visualization to become unstuck, open the way to possibilities, and activate intense desires to foment and come true. Let us begin.

CHAPTER 16

Get Unstuck: D—Desire Must Be Developed into a Plan in D.R.E.A.M.

Desire is the crucial impetus to effectively become unstuck and pursue your dreams. You must want it to the point where you almost feel it, smell it, hear it, and taste it. As I mentioned earlier, experiencing things on a multisensory level makes it even more powerful. Try the following exercise:

Visualize a future orientation of a burning desire of yours. Close your eyes for a moment and imagine your desire. Observe yourself in action. Notice your expression, your body language, your attire. If your presentation lacks confidence, correct it in your mind. Look at your location and important landmarks. Who else besides you is present? Listen to any sounds, such as a conversation you may be having with one or many people. Do you notice a distinct scent? After you imagine this, take out a notepad or journal. Write *Desire* at the top and record the visual you just experienced. If there is an emerging artist within you and drawing is your preference, go ahead and draw. Either medium can be quite effective. Now you have the desire not only crystallized in your mind, but you have it on paper to revisit at any time. Desire is not enough, however. On its own, nothing is going to happen.

You can visualize your burning desire into perpetuity, but without developing a plan, movement will not occur. D for *develop* must partner with desire as the first step for the D.R.E.A.M. to succeed. You need a mechanism to turn it into an operation. Think of it as the instrument which brings music to life. A composer may develop a beautiful tune within their mind, but without putting it on paper and allowing the musical notes to join together, the only appreciative listener is the composer. What is your instrument to develop a plan? Is it the written word, audio, video, or networking? Perhaps more than one of those venues is your modus operandi. Whatever you choose, develop your plan, do it consistently, and aim for small, steady and realistic expectations toward your goal. Maybe you do not know the best approach to take. If so, look at your desire, which you have brought to life on paper, close your eyes, and just free associate. Write those thoughts down. If nothing materializes in your mind, repeat it. I once heard a writer state that if you sit long enough in front of a blank slate, something will eventually reveal itself. I could not agree more. Once some thoughts foment, ask questions to turn those thoughts into objectives with "I will...." Maybe those thoughts will alter their composition or make room for more. Eventually, you will formulate an outline to accomplish your goals.

One of the most important factors in pursuing your desire is to seek out assistance from others, as well as using new technology. As a young and even now as a seasoned therapist, I have had supervisors, consultants, my own therapist, and peers to help me continue my development. Although the world of behavioral and mental health is a bit behind in utilizing some of the tools of technology, I have embraced them. Emailing and texting my appointments made my psychotherapy practice more efficient. No one has ever abused this system, which is often a concern for therapists. In fact, my clients were the first to alert me of the benefits using these modes of communication. Rather than play telephone tag with voicemail, a simple email or text to confirm an appointment has saved me time and money.

As I continue to develop my business as a keynote speaker and success coach, I use the services of my talented friend and strategic coach, Marilee Driscoll. In addition, periodically, I consult with the gifted Intuitive Lynn Robinson. Both of these women have provided me with guidance and ideas with immeasurable value. Along with their valuable insights, they have shared websites and Internet tools which I would never have found and which brought my business to another level. With their assistance, I avoided getting stuck. On a weekly basis, my friend and fellow speaker/coach Lisa Sasso and I confer with each other about our latest needs and happenings. We met during our Fast Track course with the National Speakers Association, of which I am a proud and grateful member. Lisa and I have turned a fortuitous monthly gathering into a nice peer relationship/ friendship. We plan on meeting with a couple of other participants from that class.

National Speakers Association provides tools for marketing our business while Toastmasters gives me the opportunity to hone my craft as a speaker. I cannot say enough about this hidden gem. This remarkable organization is for anyone who is a life-long learner, has a desire to improve their communication skills through speaking and listening, and wishes to acquire valuable constructive criticism. Not only do they support your growth in speaking confidently at the podium, decreasing your ums and ahs, and developing your extemporaneous skills, they are invaluable for those who wish to pursue leadership roles.

What is my purpose of sharing all these endeavors with you? I want to show you that developing your plan usually involves many parts which allows it to evolve into something substantive. Your plan and how it unfolds may be very different from mine. Whatever it may be, stick to it through rough times because you will have a visit from uncertainty. I know because I encounter it myself when I'm pursuing a new venture. Every so often, I silently ask, "Why am I doing this at a point in my life when many people are choosing to slow down?" During those infrequent but dubious moments, my answer to me is, "There is no alternative." In addition, I remind myself of the beautiful quotes that keep me on track. The first is by the great Napoleon Hill which I mentioned earlier and is worth repeating, "Whatever the mind can conceive and believe, it can achieve." I remind myself of this on a regular basis. The second is by the consummate master of opera, Beverly Sills, "You may be disappointed if you fail, but you are doomed if you don't try." This quote reinforces my stance of "no alternative." The great and prolific Frederick Douglass' timeless quote is never far from my mind, "Without struggle, there can be no progress." Finally, this last quote leads me back to Napoleon Hill who quotes in a similar vein, "Strength and growth come only through continuous effort and struggle."

Do you like these quotes? Do they resonate with you? If not, find your own, write them down and keep them nearby. They will be your salvation when the going gets tough. Now go ahead and begin writing some ideas to begin your plan to develop your desire.

CHAPTER 17

Get Unstuck: R—Replace, Repetition, Resilience in D.R.E.A.M.

Let us return to the topic of habits. They say, "Old habits die hard." I am sure you would agree with this idiom. Some of the issues which prevent people from getting unstuck is fear of rejection or failure and a replay of old messages such as "I can't...It is too difficult...I am too old...What if I fail...." As a result, feeling stuck prevails. If you want your desire to be developed into a plan you will want to execute, you must learn to counter unrealistic fears and self-deprecating messages. How do we do that? Well, habits are not eradicated easily, so they must often be replaced with something constructive. For example, people who habitually drink will attend many multiple AA meetings to replace a destructive behavior.

If you have difficulty thinking about how to replace bad habits, ask yourself some challenging questions. How is this new habit helpful to me? What is the worst thing that could happen? How much do I want this? The answers should help you consider a different approach. Next, you need to replace the old message with a new one, which can eventually become a new habit. A sentence as simple as "I can, and I will" combines confidence and action. It is also short and sweet and can be repeated easily, which leads us to the importance of repetition.

People often develop the habit of exercising for health, weight management, and mood alteration. Many do this on a regular basis and repeat the same exercise over and over. Eventually, this habit, if maintained, will deliver impressive results. Repetition can also be applied to changing behavior. Obviously, it is more abstract and complicated. Consequently, altering old messages and fears may be far more arduous than lifting a heavy barbell. Why? They are often imprints from long ago and changing them requires serious concentration, practice, and repetition. By repeatedly replacing the old with the new, you are also building resilience, the bulwark against challenge, struggle, and being stuck.

We are all capable of developing resilience. Some have a more natural inclination toward it, while others do not realize how resilient they are until they face adversity. What exactly is resilience? According to the FreeDictionary.com which has the simplest definition, *resilience* is: "The ability to recover quickly from illness, change, or misfortune; buoyancy." Resilience is a nice complement to tenacity. No matter how much tenacity or grit you may have, you will be tested when you fall during the topsy-turvy journey of life. Your resilience will retrieve you from such a fall. Through the repetition of positive messaging, you can build resilience.

Hopefully, you are already replacing those old debilitating messages with new empowering statements. Take those newer messages and develop a simple mantra. Prepare yourself to use it as a mind/body exercise. Look in the mirror. Notice your posture. Make sure your head is high and your shoulders are back, taking a position of openness and strength. Now give yourself a dazzling smile, which you deserve. Say your mantra such as, "I can, and I will." Perhaps another statement resonates better for you or you have one that is more specific. Whatever you choose, make sure you say it with confidence and resolve. Repeat it over and over! Remind yourself that people who participate in physical exercise strengthen their muscles. You are strengthening your mind. Do this repeatedly, when you get up, and when you go to bed. Write down your mantra so you can say it to yourself several times a day. Eventually, you will notice a shift in your thinking and self-perception. The crippling fears and messages of the past now reside resoundingly in the past. Your resilience is electrifying! There is no stopping you now!

CHAPTER 18

Get Unstuck: E—Engaging Communication is Pursuing Excellence in D.R.E.A.M.

How often do you hear the words "effective communication"? I hear them on a regular basis. When most people see these words, the first thought that comes to mind is the person's ability to speak or converse in a cogent manner. Many of us know people who present in such a way, but when you approach them, some do not even give you eye contact. They are looking around and half listening. Has that ever happened to you? I am sure most of you would nod in the affirmative. Yes, their speaking may be remarkable, but their overall communication is not. I have chosen to refer to good communication as *engaging* communication. When someone is communicating a

message, I want to feel like they are talking to me.
If I am allowed to approach the presenter, I hope to
be heard.

Communication embodies three components: speaking, writing, and listening. Of the three, listening
is heavily weighted at 40 percent, while speaking
and writing are each at 30. Listening is a major
part of my profession, and I have observed over
the years that it takes a back seat though its significance cannot be emphasized enough. Listening is
truly the understated sibling in the communication family. People do not realize how crucial it is
to be a good listener, which, sadly, many people are
not. Returning to the issue of excuses, some would
say they suffer from a diagnosis which affects their
listening abilities. My response is: If you are going
to function in our fast-paced society, you must work
on these skills. An engaging communicator learns
to not only speak effectively but to listen with
attention and focus. Like all of you, I have met and
spoken with engaged communicators who listen
intently and make you feel like you are the only
person in the room. Those presenters give you their

undivided attention, as brief as it may be. They are truly engaging communicators.

Listening is not just important for those who present. It is crucial in all areas of life. Personal and professional relationships often suffer because of one's inability to listen. Many people are great at talking about themselves but do not afford the person on the other end the same courtesy. Does it mean they have no interest? Perhaps, but even if that is not the case, one experiences it that way. Consequently, relationships get stuck, and often the non-listener is surprised when a marriage is in danger or a friendship ends. People should always be working on their listening skills.

Back in the late 1980s, a few friends and I belonged to an association where people participated in winter sports. Because I was perfectly content talking with my own friends, I did not notice that other members were less engaged. Now, these members were educated and professional. Frequently, they would participate in light bantering, but that was about it. One day during a weekend excursion, one of my astute friends, Pammie, pointed out the obvious. She said, "Darlene, do you realize none of these people ever inquire about us, even when we ask about them?" I hadn't, but I began to observe and tested it out. I would ask other members how they were doing and try to engage them. They would smile, but if I did not continue the conversation, communication would cease. Not only did they not reciprocate, but they appeared to have no interest in listening. I wonder if they were better in more intimate surroundings with close friends and family, or more attentive in a professional setting. I certainly hope so, but in these relaxed social situations, it was clear they were unable to extend themselves.

If you think about it, listening is a way to become unstuck. Keeping not only your eyes but your ears open positions you for greater awareness and engagement. Consider being a practitioner of engaged communication. You may capture opportunity knocking in a way you might have missed by not communicating in this engaged fashion.

As you may have already ascertained, not only are you getting unstuck, but by following some of these suggestions, you are pursuing excellence. There was a famous book, *In Pursuit of Excellence*, which many of you may have read. I never did, but remember the compelling title and its prominent place on the bestseller list. When we pursue any venture, it should never be done haphazardly. All of us should strive toward excellence if we wish to be the best we can be during our life's journey. Whether it be something simple or great, we need to continue to aim high. My absolute belief is by pursuing excellence we can avoid most of the pitfalls of getting stuck. Stagnation leads to stuckness, which is why so many people pursue excellence without even realizing it.

Let us examine the world of amateur sports. Consider the people who participate in marathons and triathlons, including the extremely grueling Ironman. Is that not pursuit of excellence? Are they not pushing themselves to achieve the next level? By participating in such activities, they are moving not only physically but mentally. What about people who write books and create art well into their twilight years?

By accomplishing, are they not pursuing excellence? How about people in Toastmasters? As they hear constructive criticism to promote growth, are they not constantly reaching to be a better communicator and more effective leader? There are so many examples of the benefits of approaching life in this manner, both personally and professionally. Pursuing excellence will not only help you get unstuck but assist you toward greater success. Is it no wonder I chose engaged communication and excellence for the letter *E*? Engaged communication is a pursuit of excellence. Communicating attentively and engagingly is striving to be the best you can be.

CHAPTER 19

Get Unstuck: A—Authenticity Platinum Style in D.R.E.A.M.

Not long ago, I heard the author/speaker/marketer Michael Port speak on the program Voices of Experience offered by the National Speakers Association. He talked about being our authentic selves, most importantly our best authentic selves. I thought about what he said, and it made a great deal of sense to me. I decided to take it a step further and add the label "platinum-style" authenticity because of the beauty of platinum and the exceptional value of this metal. Although it may fluctuate with the value of gold, platinum is truly the rarest of precious metals and usually placed on a higher level than gold when using a standard or award such as "the platinum package" or "the platinum record." As I mentioned earlier in this book, we should put aside our wish to be like someone else because we never can be and why would we want to be? Let us instead strive to be like that rarest of metals, shimmery and sparkling with the real, true you shining through. I am always promoting this, so just writing the suggestion makes me excited for whomever is ready to embrace it. I have come across so many people who are not comfortable enough to allow their true dazzling self to emerge. Well, if that has been you, this is your time to work on changing the narrative because you are on the path toward getting unstuck!

Now write down three of your best attributes. I repeat my earlier instructions: Do not avoid this or say you have none! After writing the attributes, look in the mirror again and say them out loud, "I am...." Give yourself another smile and do it again, and again, and again several times a day. Begin to acquaint yourself with the platinum-style authentic you who deserves to be a part of the world. Once you practice this for a while and feel comfortable, you are ready for the next step. Go ahead and introduce that magnificent, authentic part of you which has been hidden for too long!

CHAPTER 20

Get Unstuck: M—Move in D.R.E.A.M.

The last few chapters have given you examples of how to get unstuck. The word *move* could not be more fitting as a representative of the letter *M* in D.R.E.A.M. Movement is streaming through the course of your being. Although your potential has always been there, you are finally using all your talents and skills to move. Now that you are becoming unstuck and getting in touch with the remarkable you, where are you going? What might be your next step? Have you already begun to move toward greater fulfillment and contentment? If this book has helped you move, I believe you are already on your way to greater movement. Remember, as stated in so many places, success is a marathon, not a sprint, and success gives momentum to more success. Beware of those tempting quick fixes which often entice us for the faster, easier way. Recall the quotes of Frederick Douglass and Napoleon Hill before you embark on those so-called miraculous panaceas.

There is much suffering in the world, and I sympathize with those who wish for a faster approach. There are some very specific problems which can be resolved in a very timely fashion, but here we are talking about overall change in how we navigate the world around us. All of us enjoy the stimulation and flash of sparkly fireworks. They are fun and exciting, but they are evanescent. The long steady flame may be less alluring, but it is what sustains us. So many people look for fireworks throughout life, only to be consistently disappointed as they quickly become embers. The longer flame may take a while to light, but when it does how enduring it will be. Continue your movement toward that light. Do not allow the lure of fleeting fireworks seduce you from your movement toward steadfast change. Otherwise, you will become stuck again. Continue developing your desire, replacing negativity with new positivity, and repeating as you build greater resilience, pursuing excellence by becoming a more engaged communicator, and sparkling through with the platinum-style authentic you!

You are now ready to do what Luther Vandross suggested in his lively song "Ain't No Stoppin' Us Now." Many of you might recall the lyrics: "Ain't no stopping us now! We're on the move! Ain't no stopping us now! We've got the groove!" Now that you are unstuck and moving, are you ready to use your new groove? I believe you are.

All right, it is time. Put on your best attire and stand tall with majesty and grace. Look in the mirror and bestow yourself with a most dazzling smile. Simply put, you are just amazing! Are you excited to take the newer, evolving you and reveal it to others? I certainly hope so. With your new groove, go ahead. Get moving, go out and meet others, and *Stop Depriving the World of You!*

CHAPTER 21

Get Unstuck and *Stop Depriving the World of You*

Last year, I heard a fabulous quote saying the past is like a rearview mirror. Everything you see eventually shrinks and disappears before your eyes. The rest of the quote referenced the windshield. This part reminds us of the openness of the front window. This expansive window represents the future stretched in front of us. Rather than cling to the past, be ready for the excitement of the unknown, no matter how long or short this rung of the journey may be. Truly, you do not know what delights may lie ahead, even if there is hardship along the way.

When I turned 30, half a lifetime ago, I naively said to my colleagues, "I heard the 30s were the best time of your life."

One of my colleagues who was over 40 looked at me and smiled. Her response was, "They are good, but not necessarily the best."

Her message stayed with me and continued to resonate as I passed my fortieth, fiftieth and now, well, another momentous one. I remain beyond grateful I have the gift of life. In addition, my excitement about the future remains as high as it can be. Life can be quite unpredictable, and, as we age, no one knows when their time on earth is over. My continuous drive to pursue excellence is based on the very issue of life and the need to make the most of it in a positive and constructive way. Again, I reiterate: every single person who is willing to open the door to life's possibilities is capable of the same.

For those of us who have had the privilege of living this length of time, searing disappointments and losses are inevitable. When this happens, you have a choice. For the rest of your life, you can wade in the waters of unfairness, lamenting lost opportunity, or you can celebrate, take a risk, and ride the wave toward the unknown. Within reason, do not let age defy you. In addition, do not allow others to derail you because of their own fears or their discomfort with your change. Think about the discovery of the Americas. People thought the earth was flat, until Christopher Columbus stepped outside the comfort zone of conventional thinking and proved otherwise. What about you? Are you willing to take a small step outside of where you have been? I hope my book has convinced you to consider it.

Most of this book including the title *Stop Depriving the World of You* evolved from my experiences as a therapist, which I have been most of my adult life. Becoming a therapist, whether you are a Licensed Clinical Social Worker like me or part of another discipline, is not a job. Some might even say that it is not a profession but a calling. However one views the role, I believe it becomes part of your identity. People are often intrigued when you tell them the kind of work you do. There are many misconceptions about therapy, and even more about the role of clinical social workers as therapists. Without spending too much time on this, people often enter therapy to address a problem. The reasons they stay are a different story. In addition, people often assume clients must have a major mental health illness to seek psychotherapy services. In the 21st century, such a narrative is now a myth. All my lovely clients are regular people who function well in society. Psychotherapy, thankfully, has become much more mainstream and available to the everyday person.

The role of the clinical social worker has been and continues to be misconstrued. Our discipline is often ignored by the media. When discussing mental health services, media usually acknowledges only psychologists and psychiatrists. Ironically, most of the mental health services in this country have been and continue to be provided by clinical social workers. Although the understanding of our role is continuing to improve, the National Association of Social Workers needs to remain vigilant in educating and enlightening others about the amazing services provided by our profession. In fact, of all the disciplines, it is my opinion that we are the most strength-based in recognizing the resilience of the human spirit.

Over the years, the rewards of this mighty profession cannot be overstated. Words cannot express my deep appreciation and honor to be a part of so many lives. Although I have a graduate degree, along with numerous courses postgraduate, most of my learning has come from sitting with my remarkable clients. Many of these incredible people could be my friends if they were not under my professional auspices. They not only have shared their problems and secrets but their life stories and dreams. To be a trusted confidante is a most gratifying experience, and I thank my clients for having the courage to engage in a foreign process with an unknown human being. I hope I have done them well! Some have stayed with me for many years, while others do a piece of the work, often returning one, two, five, or ten years later. Although I know they have reconvened therapy because of a new conflict in their life, it is always a pleasure to see them again.

Some of my clients have been disabled, yet, like my cousin I mentioned earlier, they have attitudes that evoke images of warmth and sun. Such an outlook has helped them deal with their unfair afflictions. For many years, I worked with a lovely gentleman who became disabled as a teen. He entered therapy for reasons other than his disability, and I treated him accordingly. This man never allowed his disability to define him, nor did he ever give up hope for a medical intervention to correct it. I likened him to a warrior who was maimed in battle but continued onward and forward. Sadly, he died a few years ago. During his funeral service, being the keeper of secrets, I sat discreetly in the back of the church, tears streaming down my face. Frequently, I think of this amazing man and remind myself how much he taught me about his relentless determination to remain open to the possibilities. For him, there was no alternative. I am deeply honored to have been a small but integral part of his life, and I salute him.

The role of the therapist can be multifaceted, and for those of us who tend to be more active, we take on the role of coach. Many of the suggestions and exercises in this book have been used in some form with my clients, coaching and cheering them on. I have actively encouraged my clients to connect with others by braving into an arena of the unknown.

Their journey is a slow but steady metamorphosis of a true and glorious being. This self was always there, but needed assistance in being awakened from its cocoon to foster the transcendence of an evolved, unique person. These same people would often tell me I offered a sense of safety, which made it easier for them to take a risk and expose their authentic selves. Due to their painful histories, however, they were not so willing to chance it with the world at large. I let them know I understood and would help them fortify and ready themselves for their new course. I concurred that something would probably not change in the short term, but, although it is never guaranteed, the odds were in their favor for long-term rewards. In order to attain greater fulfillment, I repeatedly encouraged them to persevere and venture outside familiar surroundings. Emphatically, I expressed my absolute conviction that if they shared their authentic, evolved selves, then positive changes and connections would follow. In addition to my support during the session, I began offering a final cheer at the end saying: "You are depriving the world of you!" I felt so strongly about this that I started voicing it on a regular basis. As much as they enjoyed my suggestion, which I exclaimed with exuberance, something began to gnaw at me. I realized this statement wasn't enough. A word or two were definitely missing. I kept thinking about it, wondering what was needed to give it more "oomph." Mulling it over in my mind, another way to phrase the statement began to take root. I smiled as the words shifted and said to myself, *I know what I should really be saying. Yes, this is perfect, and so it began:* "Stop depriving the world of you!"

Acknowledgments

Oh my goodness, where do I begin? Well, I will start at the very beginning. I would like to thank my publisher David Wildasin for believing in me and recognizing I had the ability to write this book. I would also like to thank Christina Lynch who brought my articles to the attention of David. My gratitude to both of you cannot be put into words.

I want to thank my sisters in another life: Mary Donnelly-Barbato, Barbara Mudd, Shari Bennett, and Pam Presson. All of you have been a major part of my existence for over 30 years. I am so blessed to have had you in my life for so long. I cannot imagine this journey without any of you.

Thank you to Aunt Helen Faucher! Like my sisters above, you are truly my aunt in another life. Your warmth and love throughout the years are immeasurable.

I would like to thank the remarkable Lynne Robinson whose intuitive brilliance helped guide me on this remarkable rung of my life journey. Everyone should have a reading with Lynne!

Thank you to John Willig! You helped me navigate a whole new world of contracts and publishing. I am most grateful to you for that as well as your kindness and support.

Marilee Driscoll, the talented strategy coach, cannot be thanked enough. Without Marilee's suggestion to read Napoleon Hill and write a newsletter, I do not believe I would be writing any of this right now.

I would like to thank other old friends which include Michael, Abby, and Emily Mudd, along with newer friends Kathy McDermott, Susan Smiley, and Loret Schur, who have offered me support in both my writing and speaking endeavors. All of you are simply marvelous. I am so appreciative of being connected to you.

Thank you to my in-laws Patricia and John Hyjek for bringing my husband and his delightful sister, Jonnie-Lee des Cognets into the world. Thanks J.L. for all your support, and Pat and John, 80 is the new 60 as exemplified by you.

My friends and colleagues from my remarkable practice Needham Psychotherapy Associates cannot be overlooked, especially Tracy Welch, Naomi Litrownik, Noreen Kavanaugh, Joseph Rubin, and Andrea Masterman. You have been most supportive of my endeavors, and I cannot say thank you enough.

Thank you to the National Speakers Association at large as well as NSA New England. I cannot express enough gratitude for all of the tools you have offered in furthering my career as a speaker and author.

Thank you Lisa Sasso, my friend from Fast Track. Our weekly connection is invaluable because we help each other stay on track just like in Fast Track.

A great big shout out to my wonderful Toastmaster peers at Wachusett Toastmasters in Lancaster, Massachusetts. Toastmasters is truly a hidden gem, and our club offers so much. The belief in lifelong learning is so evident as we convene every week with enthusiasm and zeal. What a splendid group!

Thank you to the Massachusetts Chapter of the National Association of Social Workers, especially Anita Mulcahey, who encouraged me to write an article for Focus, the monthly newsletter years ago. Anita, little did you or I know, you were helping me launch my writing career.

Thank you to my fellow board members at the New England Society of Clinical Hypnosis. It has been an honor to be a part of a board of such talented and accomplished professionals. All of you are just amazing.

Finally, last but not least, I want to thank my clients who have allowed me the privilege of being the keeper of secrets. I cannot even begin to express the sheer joy of seeing you resolve issues and make way for growth and change. Every one of you is a part of my book. As I mentioned in my last chapter, you have been my greatest teachers and would be my friends if you were not my clients. Perhaps, in another life, you were or will be, and what a gift that would be.

With a smile, hug and much gratitude,

Darlene

About the Author

Darlene Corbett is a Professional Speaker, Author and Success Coach. She has been in the people business for over 30 years and fervently believes everyone is capable of getting "Unstuck." Darlene lives in central Massachusetts with her husband and their enchanting Shih Tzus, Winston and Churchill. They are the true masters of the house and dazzle anyone whom they encounter. This is Darlene's first book, and she looks forward to completing her next.